D1541295

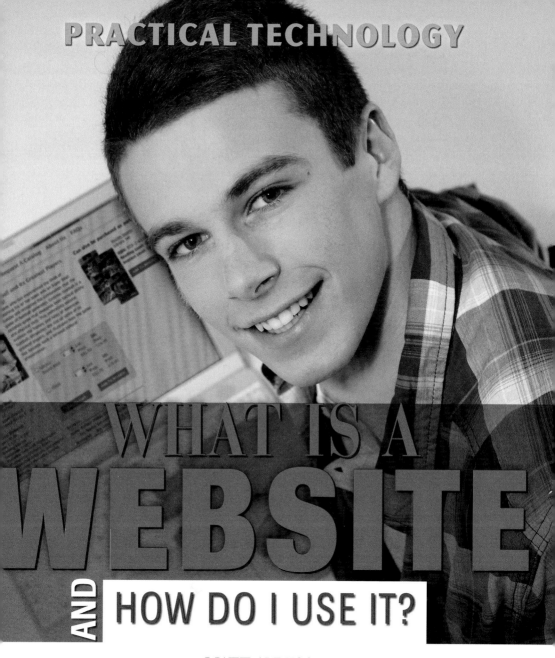

PRACTICAL TECHNOLOGY

WHAT IS A WEBSITE
AND HOW DO I USE IT?

MATT ANNISS

Britannica
Educational Publishing

IN ASSOCIATION WITH

ROSEN
EDUCATIONAL SERVICES

Published in 2014 by Britannica Educational Publishing (a trademark of Encyclopædia Britannica, Inc.) in association with The Rosen Publishing Group, Inc.
29 East 21st Street, New York, NY 10010

Distributed exclusively by Rosen Publishing.
To see additional Britannica Educational Publishing titles, go to rosenpublishing.com

First Edition

Britannica Educational Publishing
J.E. Luebering: Director, Core Reference Group
Anthony L. Green: Editor, Compton's by Britannica

Rosen Publishing
Hope Lourie Killcoyne: Executive Editor
Nelson Sá: Art Director

Library of Congress Cataloging-in-Publication Data

Anniss, Matt.
What is a website and how do I use it? / Matt Anniss. — First edition.
    pages cm. — (Practical technology)
Audience: Grade 5 to 8.
Includes bibliographical references and index.
ISBN 978-1-62275-072-6 (library binding) — ISBN 978-1-62275-073-3 (paperback) — ISBN 978-1-62275-290-4 (6 pack)
1. Web sites—Juvenile literature. 2. World Wide Web—Juvenile literature. I. Title. II. Title: What is a web site and how do I use it?
TK5105.888.A56 2014
006.7—dc23
                                    2013027170

Manufactured in the United States of America

Photo Credits
Cover: Shutterstock: Goodluz. Inside: Dreamstime: Afby71 22, Alexeysmirnov 14, Ashestosky 34, Bluelela 25, Drserg 13, Featureflash 17, Grafikszcreative 20, Guynamedjames 36, Igorborodin 30, Madmaxer 26, Mechanik 43, Miluxian 29, Monkeybusinessimages 33, 44, Pixattitude 27, Somatuscani 39, Zeber 18; Shutterstock: Alexmillos 10, Alexwhite 7, Goodluz 1, Monkey Business Images 4, Sergey Nivens 41, S Bukley 9.

CONTENTS

■ Thanks to the wonders of the World Wide Web, we can now watch videos, chat with friends, shop online, and catch up with the latest news almost wherever we are in the world.

4

INTRODUCTION

A web page is an electronic document that can be viewed by anyone with access to the Internet. Most web pages contain text and pictures. Others have audio clips, animations, video, and other interactive elements.

Web pages are organized into collections called websites. Usually, websites have a particular purpose. This might be to entertain people or to provide information. Websites can be about anything, whether it is of interest to a small group of friends or millions of people around the world.

You may have seen some web pages, perhaps when researching a school project, or just in your spare time. Websites come in many shapes and sizes, from small sites put together by teenagers to huge sites updated every day by a team of web designers and writers.

Anyone can make a web page or website. It is simple to create pages and to promote them. By the time you have finished reading this book, you should be ready to create your very own websites.

CHAPTER 1

THE WORLD WIDE WEB

Reading web pages and accessing websites is something most of us do many times a day. However, this is only possible because of the Internet—a vast system of interconnected computers and underground cables.

GLOBAL NETWORK

The Internet is a relatively new invention. During the 1960s, computer scientists figured out a way of connecting computers around the United States, and later the world, in order to exchange information more easily. Together, they worked out a system of rules, called protocols, which allowed computers to send and receive information over telephone lines.

IMPORTANT APPLICATIONS

Over time, scientists developed many different useful applications for the Internet. Some of these, such as e-mail and video conferencing systems such as Skype, have made communication easier. Others, such as file sharing, were geared toward making work easier. The Internet application that has made the greatest difference is the World Wide Web.

CHANGED LIVES

Since it was released to the general public in 1992 as a way of accessing documents electronically, the World Wide Web has changed our lives dramatically. Without the Web, we would not be able to shop online, watch videos on YouTube, or catch up with friends on social media sites such as Facebook.

Today, it is possible to buy almost anything online, from music to groceries.

All About the Web

The World Wide Web is a vast collection of electronic documents, known as web pages, stored on millions of computers around the world. Web pages can be accessed at any time of the day by anyone with a computer, tablet computer such as an iPad, or a smartphone.

Small Beginnings

The Web revolution began with a single web page, first developed in 1989 by scientists in Switzerland. The scientists used a special language they had invented called HTML (Hypertext Markup Language).

The scientists' main aim was to encourage people to use HTML to publish web pages on the Internet, where other computer users around the world could access them.

Never-Ending Growth

The idea caught on, and now there are web pages and websites on just about any subject you can think of. Whether you are interested in reading about a band such as Coldplay, your favorite football player, or the history of pizza making, you can find what you are looking for on the World Wide Web.

Web pages are packed with information. You can find out almost anything on the Web, from the latest releases by favorite bands such as Coldplay to news bulletins.

HOW BIG IS THE WEB?

No one knows exactly how many pages there are on the World Wide Web. This is because there are many different ways of indexing, or cataloging, the Web. Estimates from experts range from 1.69 billion pages to nearly 200 billion. However, all experts agree that the number of websites is increasing every day.

Web Basics

The World Wide Web may seem complicated, but the way it works is actually very simple. Here are some of the ways you can use an Internet-enabled device to find and read pages on the Internet.

Browser Basics

At their most basic, web pages are simple text files with added instructions, written in HTML. These instructions tell your device how the page is supposed to look. To view them, you need a software program called a web browser.

Server Basics

All web pages are stored on special computers called web servers. When you load a website, your browser retrieves the information directly from the web server.

When you enter an address into your browser, the browser makes a direct connection to the web server where the website you are looking for is stored.

WEB STEP BY STEP

Here is a step-by-step guide to using a web browser to access a website:

1. Open a web browser. Popular web browsers include Internet Explorer, Safari, Google Chrome, and Firefox.

2. Type in a URL (uniform resource locator). This is the website's address, for example, www.friendfeed.com. This tells your computer where to look on the Web for the page you want to access.

3. Making a connection. Your computer will now connect to the web server storing the web page.

4. Reading the HTML. Once a connection has been made, your web browser will read the HTML instructions. These instructions, known as "tags," tell your computer how to display the web page.

5. Displaying the website. Once it has read the HTML "tags," the website will appear in your web browser. You will not see these tags, as they are meant only as instructions for the browser.

CHAPTER 2

UNDERSTANDING HTML

HTML is the main structure of the World Wide Web. This computer programming language allows web developers and publishers to display content as they would like you to see it on web pages.

Tim's Big Idea

The founder of the World Wide Web and the creator of HTML is British scientist Tim Berners-Lee. In 1989, he began creating HTML as a free-to-use web publishing language. Other scientists and computer users were excited by his idea, and they soon started publishing their own web pages and websites.

Web Wars

It was not all smooth sailing in the early years of the World Wide Web. Rival companies tried to get a share of the growing web browser software market by offering different versions of HTML. In 1994, Berners-Lee started the World Wide Web Consortium (W3C) to agree to a set of standards for developers to follow. Since then, HTML has gone through many changes. The current version is called HTML5.

THE WEB BIO

Timothy Berners-Lee was born in London, England, in 1955. When he came up with the idea of a global network of electronic documents (the World Wide Web) in 1989, he had no idea how popular it would become. His HTML programming language remains the backbone of the Web.

Sir Tim Berners-Lee was knighted by Queen Elizabeth II in 2004, in recognition of his pioneering work. He is seen here at a conference in Orlando, Florida, in 2012.

HTML Basics

Creating a web page in HTML is simple thanks to HTML tags. These instructions tell a web browser how to display objects on the page, such as text and pictures.

Coded Language

If you view the source code of a web page, you can see what an HTML tag looks like. The source code shows how the page was written

■ This is what the HTML source code of a web page looks like up close. Everything enclosed within the "<" and ">" symbols is an HTML tag.

by a web developer, using HTML. You can view the source code of almost any web page using your web browser (in Internet Explorer, select the "view" menu and then click on "source").

CODED TAGS

When you look at the source code of a web page, you will notice letters or words within arrows ("<" and ">"). These letters and words contain a specific page formatting instruction in HTML code. Together, the arrows and letter or words make up an HTML tag.

HOW HTML TAGS WORK

To format a piece of text using HTML, tags must be placed at the beginning and end of the text. This is to turn the formatting "on" and "off". To make the word "dog" appear bold on a web page, you would use the following HTML code: dog

The "b" is HTML code for "bold". The "/" symbol means "end" and is used in HTML tags to turn off the formatting. On the web page, it would look like this:

Dog

FORMATTING USING HTML

The key to creating web pages using HTML is to learn the combinations of code letters and words that are inserted into tags. Once you have done this, you can use your skills to style the web page and make it look attractive.

FORMATTING OPTIONS

However you want to format your web page—from inserting pictures and video clips to adding headings and underlining key words—there are HTML tags to help you. There are around 100 HTML tags currently inuse today, although some are of limited use.

HOW TO PROCEED

You do not have to memorize all the HTML tags to create your first website. Try to at least understand what each tag will do for you. Depending upon the type of site you want to build, you may need to use only a few tags. Knowing what they all do helps you understand what else you can do with your projects. The more you experiment with tags, the easier learning HTML code will become.

COMMON HTML TAGS

To start using tags, take a look at some of the most-used HTML tags, and what they do. You can find a longer list of HTML tags at: www.w3schools.com/tags

- <b> Makes text bold.
- <center> Puts your text, images, and other elements in the center of the page.
- <font> Allows you to change the text font. The font is the basic look of the text.
- <i> Makes text italic, so that it looks like *this*.
- <img> Inserts an image.
- <url> Inserts a link to another web page. Website viewers click on the link to be taken to that page.

The <img> HTML tag allows you to insert pictures of favorite singers, such as Rhianna, onto your web pages.

CASCADING STYLE SHEETS

Designing a website with many web pages using HTML tags can be time consuming. To ensure that the look of every page remains the same, developers use Cascading Style Sheets (CSS).

LOOK AND CONTENT

CSS separate the look of a website from the content. By using CSS, designers can apply the same standard style elements, such as fonts, colors, and headings, to thousands of web pages.

When setting up CSS, web designers use normal HTML tags and codes. Once the web designers have completed the tags and codes, they are merged into a single block of HTML code that can be used throughout the website.

INTERNAL OR EXTERNAL?

There are two ways of using CSS. The first is called Internal CSS. With this method, all of the website's styling information is included in the source code at the top of each page. In External CSS, the website's styling information is contained within a single file stored on the site's web server. A link to this file is included in the source code of each individual web page.

news   about us   contacts   references   ♻ works   support   FAQ

n the Block   Bringing dance to the streets

On the Block and shake
p with other dancers.
k here to find your local
up and meeting times.

 Video If you aren't sure if dance
is your thing, have a look
at these clips to see what
others are doing and how
dance has helped them.

news

Some of our top dancers were invited
to perform in an exhibition on the
streets of New York City – click on
this tab to see what happened.

news

There are now 1,000 dancers
On the Block! Join a group and
watch this figure rise.

news

Download some of the latest dance
tracks here – you can just listen to
them, too.

more   more   more

Web designers use CSS to ensure that each page looks
the same. This means that even if the website has
hundreds of pages, they will all have the same look.

 Do Running Man: watch
this video to find out how.

☆ Do Doughie: watch this
video to find out how.

☆ Do Spongebob: watch this
video to find out how.

TABLES AND FRAMES

As HTML has developed, it has become easier to create great looking websites using more complicated features. Two of the most popular tools are tables and frames.

TABLE TURNING

Tables allow designers to arrange a number of images, features, or blocks of text into a grid formation. They can then display a lot of different content at once. A good example of a table in action can be found on the Nickleodeon website (www.nick.com), which features a grid of squares roughly the same size.

If you look at the web page below, you will see that it is arranged neatly and follows a rough grid. This effect is created by using tables and frames.

YourSite

Sign Up!

★ GREETING'S ★

search...

| HOME | ABOUT | PRODUCTS | SERVICES | GALLERY | CONTACT |

"Adventure is Out There!"

IN THE FRAME

Frames allow designers to "frame" the content of their pages with features that remain the same throughout a website. The content in the frames around the edge of the page stay the same, whichever page readers are viewing.

MAKING AN HTML TABLE

Using just four tags, HTML designers can create a simple table. The four tags are: <table>, <th> (table header), <tr> (table row), and <td> (table data). Here's the code to create the table below:

```
<table>
<tr>
<th>Header 1</th>
<th>Header 2</th>
</tr>
<tr>
<td>cell 1</td>
<td>cell 2</td>
</tr>
</table>
```

Viewed on a website, the code looks like this:

Header 1	Header 2
cell 1	cell 2

HTML5 makes it easier for web designers to create interactive pages. They can even broadcast live footage of extreme sports, such as skateboarding.

HTML5

As the World Wide Web has evolved, so has the HTML used to create web pages.

TOOLS OF THE TRADE

HTML5 gives web page developers the tools to create websites that almost leap off the computer screen. It can do this because it uses something called an Application Program Interface (API). This is a set of tools for creating interactive websites.

HTML5's API, which is called DOM (Document Object Model), provides web designers with the building blocks to create amazing pages and sites.

Special Features

The API used in HTML5 makes it much easier to include music and videos in websites. It also allows web designers to create their own HTML tags using a new computer language called Extensible Markup Language (XML). Before XML, designers had to work with a limited set of options. Now, almost anything is possible.

HTML5 AT WORK

To understand how HTML5 has changed the Internet, compare one of today's best interactive pages with the world's first website. You will be amazed at the difference!

THEN
info.cern.ch/hypertext/WWW/TheProject.html

NOW
www.scienceofeverydaylife.com

What's New with HTML5?

HTML5 is a giant leap forward for website design. Its range of new features makes it easier than ever before for people with little or no technical knowledge to create fun, great-looking websites.

Style Elements

The features used in HTML5 are known as "elements." There are a number of new elements in HTML5, such as the canvas element. This allows designers to draw graphics (see page 25). HTML5 has also updated features previously seen in HTML, such as the ability to create forms and tables.

Fun Elements

Two of HTML5's most important features are the "audio element" and the "video element." These allow designers to include music and video clips. Before HTML5, music and video could only be added using special applications called "plug-ins." Not all web browsers supported these plug-ins, which could be frustrating for website visitors. However, with HTML5, plug-ins are rarely needed.

INTERACTIVE ELEMENTS

One of the original HTML plug-ins is a programming language called JavaScript. This was used to add interactive content. JavaScript is now included in HTML5, and is used in one of HTML5's best new features, the "canvas element." This feature gives designers greater control over the look of their websites by allowing them to draw colored shapes directly onto a web page.

Using the canvas element, web developers are able to add features such as the speech bubble and photo-frame effect shown on this website.

CHAPTER 3

WEB SERVERS

So far, we have looked at how web developers use HTML code to design and format websites. But how are Internet users able to view the sites that the developers have created?

FILE UPLOAD

Once a designer or developer has finished a web page or website, he or she must place it on the Internet so that it can be accessed by other people. To do this, the designer must transfer or upload the finished electronic pages, called files, to a storage computer known as a web server. If the website has a lot of files, these are often organized into different storage spaces, called folders, on the web server.

UNIVERSAL LANGUAGE

Once a website has been uploaded, it is given a unique website address, known as a URL. The URL is the electronic equivalent of a business address.

Internet users can then access the website or web page by entering the URL into the address bar of a web browser such as Internet Explorer or Firefox.

WHAT'S IN A URL?

We have all seen website addresses, but what do they mean? Let's look at this URL to find out! http://www.foxnews.com/sports/football

[http] This is an acronym of HyperText Transfer Protocol. It is a communication code that allows computers to exchange information. This part of the address tells the computer to make a connection to the web server using "HTTP."

[www.foxnews.com] This is the main part of the "URL." The "www" shows that it is part of the World Wide Web, while "foxnews.com" is the website's unique address, sometimes known as a domain name.

[/sports] This is the folder on the foxnews.com web server, where the web page is located.

[/football] This is the web page file where the football news is kept.

By using the URL for a news agency, you can go straight to the football pages.

INTERNET ADDRESSES

The World Wide Web is like a huge electronic mail system. Information is mailed back and forth between computers and web servers. This is done using a system called Internet Protocol, or "IP."

VIRTUAL STREET ADDRESS

Every electronic device with Internet access, from web servers and home computers to smartphones and tablet computers such as iPads, is given its own unique "IP address." This is a long series of numbers (for example: 82.33.117.166) used to identify the specific computer or server. Much like the URL, the IP address, too, is like a virtual street address.

WHAT'S MY IP ADDRESS?

Unless you are a computer expert, you probably will not know the IP address of your home computer or tablet. It is possible to find out, though, by visiting this website: www.whatismyipaddress.com/ip-lookup. This site automatically finds your computer's IP address when you connect to it.

The IP address for the social network Twitter is 199.59.150.7, but we know it by its domain name, which is www.twitter.com.

Domain Name

It is difficult for us to remember long IP addresses, so web servers are given human-friendly "domain names," such as twitter.com. When a website is first placed on the Internet, its domain name is linked to the IP address of its web server by special computers called Domain Name Servers (DNS). This is how your web browser knows exactly which IP address to connect to when you type in a website's URL.

Ports and Protocols

IP addresses help computers make connections to web servers. However, to get or retrieve web pages, they need to be able to talk the same language. How exactly do they do this?

Universal Language

The language of the World Wide Web is called HyperText Transfer Protocol, or "HTTP." This is a set of rules, known as protocols, that allow web browsers to request access to a website, and receive the information needed to correctly display the pages.

Web pages are sent back and forth using a special computer language known as HyperText Transfer Protocol (HTTP).

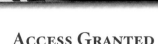

ACCESS GRANTED

There is one last piece of the jigsaw: ports. These are the channels on the web server that a computer uses to access the website the user wants to view. If the web server's IP address is its "home address," then the port is the "front door" that a browser uses to access the website.

HTTP MADE EASY

Every time a computer makes a request to access a website, it sends a message like this, using HTTP, to the web server:

GET / HTTP/1.1
Host: www.simple-help.com

This means "get me www.simple-help.com, I am using HTTP." The web server will respond with a message like this:

HTTP/1.1 200
Content-type: text/html
Content-length: 1020

This means: "OK, it's a web page, it's this long, here it is." The page will then be transferred to the web browser.

Server-Side Technology

It is not just HTML5 that has allowed website designers to create fantastic, interactive websites. The development of "server-side technology" has also played a key role.

Role Reversal

Server-side technology gives website users greater control over the content of websites. It tailors what is displayed to users' interests or demands by using a combination of programming languages and systems developed for use in HTML5 such as XML, ASP (Active Server Pages), PHP (HyperText Preprocessor), and SQL (Structured Query Language). These are all designed to vary the content of websites depending on a user's demands.

Different Process

Traditionally, websites are retrieved from the web server and displayed as they were designed. However, server-side technology helps designers to create pages that include many different elements by using several systems. The server-side software brings all these elements together, arranges them, and then sends the browser detailed instructions.

SERVER-SIDE SITES

Social networks such as Facebook and Twitter use server-side technology to show content that is tailored to individual users based on their interests or with whom they are friends. YouTube uses similar technology to tailor video "recommendations" to the interests of users.

Social network sites such as Facebook use server-side technology to suggest new friends who share the user's interests, such as football, pop music, and movies.

CHAPTER 4

PROMOTING WEBSITES

With millions of websites online, making a website stand out from the crowd can be tough. Thankfully, there are plenty of ways to promote a website to help increase visitor numbers.

Meta than the Rest

Most web designers use meta tags to help promote their websites. These are special HTML tags that include a description of a website's content as well as a list of key words associated with what it contains.

Love Meta

Meta tags are usually hidden from regular website visitors. Instead, they are inserted into the page's source code.

This means that the meta tags will be picked up when someone performs a web search, using a search engine such as Google or Bing.

UNDERSTANDING META TAGS

If you look at the source code of a website (see pages 14–15), you should find the page's meta tags at the top of the page, in the "header" (introduced by the <head> HTML tag). There are three main parts to every meta tag:

- Description—This is a brief description of the website and what it's about.
- Keywords—A list of words associated with the website's content.
- Author—The name of whoever made the website.

Here's an example of a meta tag for an imaginary website about hip-hop culture and rap music, in HTML code:

```
<head>
<meta name="description" content="Hip-hop culture website">
<meta name="keywords" content="rap music,breakdancing,hip-hop,beatboxing,turntablism">
<meta name= "author" content="DJ Made-Up and Imaginary MC">
</head>
```

Search engines such as Google have built up enormous catalogues of websites, allowing users to find MP3 tracks of popular songs within a matter of seconds.

SEARCH ENGINES

It can be challenging to remember more than a handful of website addresses. Luckily, search engines and directories can help, much like an address book or an encyclopedia.

SEEKING ANSWERS

Search engines are websites that allow users to find pages relevant to topics they are interested in. Search engines such as Google and Bing use computer programs called crawlers to search the Web, cataloging the contents of websites.

Finding Results

When people use a search engine, they are not actually searching the World Wide Web but rather the search engine's catalog of websites. Search results are ranked according to how relevant the search engine thinks they are, with the most relevant at the top of the page.

More Answers

Search engines are just one way of finding information and promoting websites. Web directories, such as Yahoo! are also popular. These list websites by topics or categories, and include a brief description. They are more selective than search engines.

SEARCH ENGINE OPTIMIZATION

To attract more visitors to their websites, web designers use a range of techniques called Search Engine Optimization (SEO). The idea is to guarantee a high ranking for sites on search results so they are accessed more regularly. You can find out more about SEO at www. searchengineland.com/guide/what-is-seo.

CHAPTER 5

MOBILE WEBSITES

Mobile technology has changed people's lives so much in recent years by helping them stay connected to the Internet 24 hours a day, seven days a week. It has also changed the way web developers create their websites.

WEB REVOLUTION

When the World Wide Web first took off in the mid-1990s, most people thought they would be restricted to accessing websites on computer screens. Now, it is possible to surf the Web on a wide variety of portable devices, from smartphones to tablet computers and handheld game consoles.

HIT OR MISS

If you have ever tried to surf the web using a smartphone, for example an iPhone, you will know that it can be a hit-or-miss experience. Some websites can be hard to read or they do not fit properly on the phone's small screen. Others fit perfectly and look very good because they have been designed with portable devices in mind.

MOBILE CHALLENGE

Websites designed to look good on portable devices are known as mobile-enhanced websites. Designing mobile-enhanced websites is a challenge for web designers because they have to present the information in a way that will look good on many different devices, regardless of the screen size.

Companies such as Google now offer their search engines as specially designed phone applications or apps.

Design and Technology

The limitations of smartphones have forced designers to re-think the way they create sites. As a result, website technology is changing all the time.

Problems and Solutions

The wide variety of smartphones available makes designing mobile-enhanced websites challenging. Even the largest smartphone screens are no more than four inches (10 cm) high. Most screens are too small to display conventional websites without a lot of awkward zooming and scrolling.

Website designers have overcome these problems by creating websites that adapt to each type of device. They have also created mobile-enhanced sites that use simple, one-column layouts.

Automatic Recognition

Designers also use CSS (see page 18) tailored to different devices. Many sites automatically detect the type of device being used to access a website and then decide which CSS to use to display the content. If you have access to a computer and smartphone, look at the same website on each device to see the differences.

Many websites can now automatically detect the type of device being used to access their pages, for example a tablet computer such as an iPad or a smartphone, and then decide exactly how to best display the content.

Pros and Cons

Web designers have learned to work around the disadvantages of designing for small-screen smartphones, while using the phones' advantages to help them create vibrant mobile-enhanced websites.

Some Disadvantages

In addition to the difficulties of small smartphone screens, there are other problems for web designers to overcome, as well. Some plug-ins used to display interactive website content are not compatible with mobile devices. As a result, many web designers offer users specially designed smartphone apps as an alternative to mobile-enhanced sites. Users then download the apps to access the information.

More Advantages

For all the disadvantages of designing websites for smartphones and tablets, mobile devices are not all bad for web designers. Many features of today's touchscreen-enabled smartphones can be used to enhance the website viewing experience. For example, users can touch, swipe, or pinch the screen to zoom in and out of websites, or to make the text larger.

LOCATION, LOCATION, LOCATION

All modern smartphones include something called a GPS receiver. This automatically works out the phone's location by connecting to the Global Positioning System—a network of space satellites orbiting the Earth. Some of the best mobile-enhanced websites utilize the phone's GPS receiver to display content based on the user's location (for example, details of restaurants, stores, or attractions nearby).

Many websites make use of GPS technology, which is found on devices such as smartphones and tablets.

WORLD WIDE WONDER

The World Wide Web has revolutionized people's lives, putting almost endless amounts of information at their fingertips.

FREE AND EASY

One of the most exciting things about the World Wide Web is that it is available to anyone with Internet access, often free of charge. This means that anyone can create his or her own websites, upload them to a server, and invite the world to take a look.

DO IT YOURSELF

If this book has inspired you, why not try creating your own websites? There is plenty of information online, and some helpful links throughout this book.

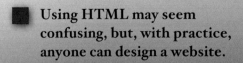

Using HTML may seem confusing, but, with practice, anyone can design a website.

TOP TIPS FOR USING WEBSITES

1. Learn new words and play word games at Word Central: www.wordcentral.com.
2. Find out the smartest ways to do a websearch with these tips for "smarter searching": www.dke-encyc.com/youandinternet. asp#topsearchtips.
3. The Web is a great place for sharing your favorite photos and videos. There are many sites to choose from, including Pinterest: www.pinterest.com.
4. If you would like to be a moviemaker, shoot some video on your smartphone and start your own web TV channel at YouTube: www.youtube.com.
5. Take an HTML tutorial and learn how to make your first website. This step-by-step guide is a great place to start: www.w3schools.com/html.
6. Learn the basics of building a website by creating your own blog. Start here: learn.wordpress.com/get-started.

API Acronym for Application Program Interface—a set of routines and tools for building software for a computer program or website.

ASP Acronym for Active Server Pages—a piece of software, based on a web server, that generates web pages, based on the requests of web users.

crawlers Computer software used by search engines to gather and update data.

CSS Acronym for Cascading Style Sheets—a feature that gives web designers and users more control over how pages are displayed.

HTML Acronym for Hypertext Markup Language—the system for creating web pages on the World Wide Web.

HTML5 An advanced version of HTML that allows web designers greater control over the look, feel, and content of their websites.

HTTP Acronym for HyperText Transfer Protocol—a tool that allows computers to exchange information and access websites.

IP address Short for Internet Protocol Address—numbers that identify devices connected to the Internet.

JavaScript A system for creating interactive content on web pages.

meta tags HTML tags used to provide information about the content of a web page or website.

search engine A website used to search the World Wide Web for references to particular topics or words.

smartphone A cell phone that has computing abilities such as Internet connectivity.

source code A set of instructions and commands that tell a computer program how to operate, or a web browser what information to display.

tags Instructions in the HTML source code of a website.

URL Acronym for uniform resource locator—the address of a specific website or file on the Internet.

web browser A computer program used to access and view websites.

web page A document that can be viewed using a web browser.

web server An online computer used for storing a website.

websites Collections of documents, known as web pages, organized into one coherent online whole.

Books

Connolly, Sean. *The Internet and the World Wide Web* (Getting the Message). Mankato, MN: Smart Apple Media, 2010.

MacDonald, Matthew. *Creating a Website: The Missing Manual*. Sebastopol, CA: O'Reilly Media, 2011.

McHarry, Sarah. *WordPress To Go: How To Build A WordPress Website On Your Own Domain, From Scratch, Even If You Are A Complete Beginner*. CreateSpace Independent Publishing Platform, 2013.

Poolos, J. *Designing, Building, and Maintaining Web Sites* (Digital and Information Literacy). New York, NY: Rosen Central, 2010.

Websites

Due to the changing nature of Internet links, Rosen Publishing has developed an online list of websites related to the subject of this book. This site is updated regularly. Please use this link to access the list:

http://www.rosenlinks.com/ptech/web